D1251607

BOOK ANALYSIS

By Lucy Meekley

Life of Pi

BY YANN MARTEL

Bright
≡Summaries.com

YANN MARTEL

SPANISH-BORN CANADIAN NOVELIST

- **Born in Salamanca, Spain in 1963.**
- **Notable works:**
  - *Self* (1996), novel
  - *Beatrice and Virgil* (2010), novel
  - *The High Mountains of Portugal* (2016), novel

Yann Martel is an award-winning Canadian novelist. His parents were members of the Canadian Foreign Service, so the family led a fairly nomadic life during his childhood, living in France, Spain and Costa Rica. He now lives in Saskatchewan, Canada. He started writing while studying Philosophy at the University of Trent, and after traveling extensively and having several different jobs, by age 27 he had made writing his career. He published several short stories in the early 1990s, which were well-received, before publishing his first novel *Self* in 1996. He shot to fame when his second novel, *Life of Pi*, won the 2002 Man

Booker Prize. Martel has been praised for his allegorical style and his highly original approach to common themes.

LIFE OF PI

AN ALLEGORICAL TALE OF SURVIVAL

- **Genre:** novel
- **Reference edition:** Martel, Y. (2003) *Life of Pi*. Canongate Books Ltd.
- **1st edition:** 2001
- **Themes:** survival, religion, storytelling, loneliness, grief

Narrated by Piscine "Pi" Molitor Patel, *Life of Pi* tells the story of a 16-year-old boy lost at sea for 227 days. Piscine's family are zookeepers who decide to immigrate to Canada, moving their animals with them. When their ship meets with disaster, only Pi and a small group of animals – including a Bengal tiger – survive, adrift at sea in a lifeboat. The novel is part adventure story and part philosophical meditation on grief, loneliness, storytelling and belief. Martel prefaces the book with a half-true anecdote about the story's genesis: his first published novel had been unsuccessful, so he flew to Bombay, India, to finish writing his second novel, where he met a man who told him "I have a story that will make you believe in God" (p. x). Whether or not that is true, it sets the tone for the novel, which explores the nature of belief and the power of the narratives we tell ourselves. Initially rejected by five publishers, the book went on to spend 61 weeks on the *New York Times* Bestseller List, and has been published in over 40 countries.

SUMMARY

LIFE AT THE ZOO

The novel begins with an author's preface, explaining that this is a true story that he heard while travelling in India. The novel is told from the point of view of Pi, recounting the remarkable events that happened to him, though the fictional author's voice interjects now and then. The opening line reads, "My suffering left me sad and gloomy" (p. 1).

Pi grows up Pondicherry, India, where his parents run a zoo. He describes growing up in a zoo as "Paradise on earth" (p. 14). He becomes fascinated by religion even as a child, despite his parents' secularism. His first becomes a Hindu, after his Auntie Rohini takes him to a temple as an infant. After visiting a Catholic church years later on a family holiday, Pi decides to become a Christian as well as a Hindu. Then, aged 15, he meets a Muslim baker and is so impressed by his prayer style that he adds Islam to his arsenal of religions. Pi does not see any problem with his

Omnist belief system, as he sees belief as one of life's most important features. Because of this, he explains that he prefers atheism to agnosticism, as agnostics "to the very end [of their life], lack imagination and miss the better story" (p. 22).

One day while walking with his family, Pi is unlucky enough to encounter all three of his religious teachers at once. They are all surprised and offended that Pi has been following three separate faiths, and everyone but Pi agrees he must choose one. Pi disagrees, countering "I just want to love God" (p. 54). In the 1970s, following widespread political unrest, the family decide to move to Canada. They sell many of their animals, but take some with them on their voyage across the Pacific.

LOST AT SEA

"The ship sank" (p. 121) is the enigmatic beginning to the next part of the story. Pi is in a lifeboat in the middle of a storm, calling for Richard Parker, the peculiarly named tiger from the family zoo, to climb aboard. One of the ship's engines has exploded in the middle of the night and some sailors have thrown Pi into a lifeboat. His family were still sleeping while this happened, and his only companions are a zebra, a hyena, Richard Parker, and they are soon joined by Orange Juice the orangutan. After a couple of days, the hyena has eaten the zebra and orangutan. Pi finds a chest of supplies on the boat, including food, water and various survival tools. He builds a raft with these supplies, while Richard Parker is distracted eating the hyena.

After debating whether he should kill the tiger, or just try to outlast him, Pi realises that the only solution is to tame him. He devises lots of strategies to keep them both alive with food and fresh water. Pi experiences extreme emotional turmoil throughout the journey, and prays often. His emotions range from hope to hopelessness, from boredom to paralysing fear. After a long stretch of time, Pi goes blind and starts to become delirious. He believes he comes across another blind man lost at sea, who he converses with. The man tries to eat Pi, but as soon as he steps into the territory of Richard Parker he is devoured. Martel does not make it explicit that this episode did not really happen, but it seems that it is a hallucination brought on by the extreme exhaustion, hunger and thirst Pi is experiencing.

This uncertain grip on reality only intensifies, as Pi then comes across an island made of algae. The island is populated by meerkats, and has freshwater ponds. Pi stays there for a while, eating the vegetation while he and Richard Parker grow stronger. It seems almost idyllic, until Pi discovers a tree at the centre of the island which has human teeth hanging from its branches instead of fruit. He realises that the algae covering the island is carnivorous and decides to leave. Eventually, the boat reaches land, which turns out to be Mexico. Richard Parker walks off into the jungle, and Pi is hurt that the tiger does not make any farewell gesture. Pi is discovered by some women from a nearby town and taken to hospital.

TWO STORIES

Pi is visited in hospital by two detectives, Mr Okamoto and Mr Chiba, who are investigating the sinking of the ship. They interview Pi and he tells them his story, but they do not believe him. Pi tells them another, much more horrifying version of the story, where instead of the animals, he is stranded on the life raft with his mother, a cook and a sailor. The cook eventually murders his mother, and Pi in turn murders the cook and eats his flesh. The detectives are horrified, but still doubtful. Pi asks:

> "In both stories the ship sinks, my entire family dies, and I suffer."
> "Yes, that's true."
> "So tell me, since it makes no factual difference to you and you can't prove the question either way, which story do you prefer? Which is the better story, the story with animals or the story without animals?"
> Mr. Okamoto: "That's an interesting question..."
> Mr. Chiba: "The story with animals." Mr. Okamoto: "Yes. The story with animals is the better story."
> Pi Patel: "Thank you. And so it goes with God."
> (p. 433)

The reader is left unsure of what version of events to believe, in keeping with the questions about the nature of belief raised earlier in the book.

CHARACTER STUDY

PISCINE (PI) MOLITOR PATEL

Martel focuses more on ideas than characters, which means that, although Pi is a likeable and funny character, he is not particularly complex. He functions instead as a mouthpiece for the philosophical ideas Martel wants to explore.

We see Pi, who is named after his parents' favourite swimming pool in France, through the lens of the imaginary author who interjects at various points in the novel. We are not told much about his life as an adult, in the aftermath of the events of the story, other than that he is married, likes spicy food and studied religion and zoology at the University of Toronto.

There are two key elements to Pi's character: his practical, empirical side, which allows him to use his knowledge to tame Richard Parker and survive on the boat, and his spiritual side, which sustains his hope during the bleak experience.

Pi's Omnism is perhaps his most prominent character feature. His first religion is Hinduism, but he does not see this as a limiting factor, and he adds Christianity and Islam to his beliefs as he grows older. He uses important lessons from each religion during his experience on the boat.

RICHARD PARKER (THE TIGER)

The character of Richard Parker can be interpreted in two ways, depending on which of Pi's stories you choose to believe. He gets his strange name from an administrative error, when a mistake on some paperwork means he ends up with the name of the hunter who captured him. He name is a literary reference to a novel by Edgar Allan Poe (American writer, 1809-1849), called *The Narrative of Arthur Gordon Pym of Nantucket* (1938).

When Pi tells the second version of his second story to the Japanese investigators, they guess that each of the animal characters represents a human character. In this case, Richard Parker is supposed to represent Pi himself. There are many instances when the distinctions between them are blurred. For example, in the way they eat:

> "I noticed, with a pinching of the heart, that I ate like an animal, that this noisy, frantic unchewing wolfing-down of mine was exactly the way Richard Parker ate." (p. 225)

In this interpretation, the relationship between Pi and the tiger can be seen as a symbolic struggle between an individual and their inner demons. In other words, Pi is trying to tame the animalistic qualities inside himself. If we believe instead that Richard Parker is a real tiger – and Martel gives us plenty of descriptive detail to justify this interpretation – he acts as a deadly but important companion for Pi on their voyage. Although Pi is terrified of the tiger, he also is in awe of him, and feels less alone in his presence. He is even sad when Richard Parker fails to make any kind of farewell gesture when they part.

THE OTHER SURVIVORS

- **Orange Juice the orangutan/Pi's mother:** when Orange Juice floats to Pi's lifeboat on a raft of bananas, it is a joyful moment. Pi says "She came floating on an island of bananas in a halo of light, as lovely as the Virgin Mary" (p. 111). This connection with the Virgin Mary reinforces the link between the orangutan and Pi's mother. Both are gentle, warm characters who attempt to stand their ground, but are ultimately not strong enough to defend themselves. They are intended to evoke a strong pang of sympathy and sadness in the reader.

- **The hyena/the cook:** the hyena represents pure, amoral instinct for survival. The cook and the hyena are ruthless in their quest to live, and eat the other characters one by one until they are eventually killed by Richard Parker/Pi. In the version of events involving the humans, the actions of the cook are more horrifying, because they break the moral codes we expect humans to abide by, whereas these actions seem more natural in animals. Pi has some respect for the cook, and even lets himself be persuaded to eat some human flesh the cook has prepared.

- **The zebra/the sailor:** the zebra is doomed from the start when it tries to jump onto the lifeboat and breaks its leg, leaving it weak. It is eventually eaten alive by the hyena and then finally killed by Richard Parker. The function of this character appears to be to highlight different attitudes to suffering and survival. His lack of resilience makes him first to be picked off by the other characters.

ANALYSIS

CONTEXT AND GENRE

Set in India the 1960s/70s, the events of *Life of Pi* take place in the period known as 'the Emergency'. In 1975, Prime Minister Indira Gandhi (Indian Prime Minister, 1917-1984) was embroiled in a corruption scandal, calling the legitimacy of her election into question. There were widespread protests against her across the country, but instead of resigning as the people wished, Gandhi declared a state of emergency. This gave her absolute power to rule, and to suspend the powers and rights stated in the constitution. This lasted until 1977. This is the context in which Pi's family are running their zoo. Pi's father, who considers himself modern and liberal, feels uncomfortable that his liberties are being curtailed, and is afraid that economic sustainability will be threatened. The family decide to immigrate to Canada.

In terms of literary context, Martel borrows features from various genres. It is, in part, an adventure story, reminiscent of *Moby Dick* (1851) or *Robinson Crusoe* (1719). Martel blends realism – sparing no details when it comes to graphic violence – with fantasy elements, such as the seaweed island and the blind Frenchman. This is a feature of the magical realism genre, pioneered by the likes of Salman Rushdie (British-Indian novelist, 1947-present) and Gabriel García Marquez (Colombian novelist, 1927-2014). Writing in this style allows Martel to constantly push the boundaries of what the reader believes. The self-conscious nature of the way the story is told, with the layering of the narrative making us conscious of the fact we are being told a story, is also a feature of Postmodernist literature. Martel blends these three genres to powerful effect, and the constant literary references throughout the novel reinforce the fact that Martel is concerned with the telling and retelling of versions of stories.

RELIGION AND SPIRITUALITY

Life of Pi is an almost biblical story about an extreme test of faith in the face of extraordinary events. As previously discussed, Pi is a deeply religious character. He follows three religions –

Hinduism, Christianity, and Islam – and beli
he does not have to choose just one (despite
protestations of his parents and religious teachers) because all he cares about is loving God.
He explains his perspective through an anecdote:

> "I know a woman here in Toronto who is very
> dear to my heart. [...] Though she has lived
> in Toronto for over thirty years, her French-
> speaking mind still slips on occasion on the
> understanding of English sounds. And so, when
> she first heard of Hare Krishnas, she didn't hear
> right. She heard "Hairless Christians", and that is
> what they were to her for many years. When I
> corrected her, I told her that in fact she was not
> so wrong; that Hindus, in their capacity for love,
> are indeed hairless Christians, just as Muslims, in
> the way they see God in everything, are bearded
> Hindus, and Christians, in their devotion to God,
> are hat-wearing Muslims." (p. 50)

He is explaining here that the differences
between the religions are trivial - almost comical
- and in essence they are all moving toward the
same end goal. From Hinduism, he takes the idea
that God is around us, within everything. This
is why he is still able to see the natural beauty
of the world when he is on his gruelling voyage.

From Christianity, he takes the human element, saying of Jesus: "what kind of god is that? It's a god on too human a scale, that's what" (p. 27). His Christian beliefs help him to deal with his own suffering. Finally, his faith in Islam, which he describes as a religion of "brotherhood and devotion" (p. 67), helps him to overcome his fear of Richard Parker and come to treat him as a companion.

Pi seems to take the best from all three religions, forming his own unique perspective on spirituality, which sees him through his ordeal. On the other hand, if we choose to believe Pi's horrifying second version of events, what role does Pi's faith play? In this case, it could be said to function as a way to tell beautiful stories that conceal and ease the pain and cruelty of reality.

NARRATIVE PERSPECTIVE

Martel chooses a complex layering of narrative to tell his story. The novel begins with a semi-true note by the author, which begins with him explaining the circumstances of how he came to be writing his second novel in India. He then begins to weave fiction into his words, telling the story of how he came across a man in India who told him about Pi's story. From the very beginning, the reader is unsure of what is fact and what is fiction, setting the tone for the whole novel.

The novel begins from Pi's perspective, but the older version of himself, many years after the events of the story. The beginning is unusual, starting with the intriguing statement "My suffering left me sad and gloomy" (p. 3) but, instead of elaborating, Pi then goes into great detail about a sloth he studied at university. Chapter 2 is written, instead, by the fictional 'author' we encountered in the initial author's note. This chapter consists of only a few lines, and is heavily elliptical in style, especially compared with the loquacious first chapter:

> "He lives in Scarborough. He's a small, slim man-no more than five foot five. Dark hair, dark eyes. Hair greying at the temples. Can't be older than forty. Pleasing coffee-coloured complexion. Mild fall weather, yet puts on a big winter parka with fur-lined hood for the walk to the diner." (p. 7)

This gives the impression more of note-taking, as though the author does not want to interfere too much with the narrative, just giving the bare contextual details. This is an artificial guise, however, as we are now aware that the story is being told through the lens of the fictional author, not by Pi directly, despite being written in first person. This ambiguous narrative style is part of Martel's wider point: that the raw facts are not important, but rather that it is the story itself and how we choose to interpret it that matters.

FURTHER REFLECTION

SOME QUESTIONS TO THINK ABOUT...

- How does the film adaptation compare to the book? Are there any differences?
- Which literary references feature in the book? What is their significance?
- Which of Pi's two stories do you believe and why?
- Pi follows three different religions. How is religion significant in the story?
- How has this experience shaped Pi as an adult?
- One of the many messages of *Life of Pi* is a defence of zoos. What argument does Pi make in favour of zoos, and how does it relate to the story more broadly?
- What does the tiger, Richard Parker, symbolise?
- Could the novel be considered a Bildungsroman (coming of age story)?

We want to hear from you!
Leave a comment on your online library
and share your favourite books on social media!

FURTHER READING

REFERENCE EDITION

- Martel, Y. (2003) *Life of Pi*. Edinburgh: Canongate Books Ltd.

REFERENCE STUDIES

- (No date) Biography: Yann Martel. *British Council of Literature*. [Online]. [Accessed 23 November 2018]. Available from: <https://literature.britishcouncil.org/writer/yann-martel>

ADAPTATIONS

- *Life of Pi*. (2010) [Film]. Ang Lee. Dir. United States: 20th Century Fox.

www.brightsummaries.com

Ebook EAN: 9782808015899

Paperback EAN: 9782808015905

Legal Deposit: D/2018/12603/537

Cover: © Primento

Digital conception by Primento, the digital partner of
publishers.